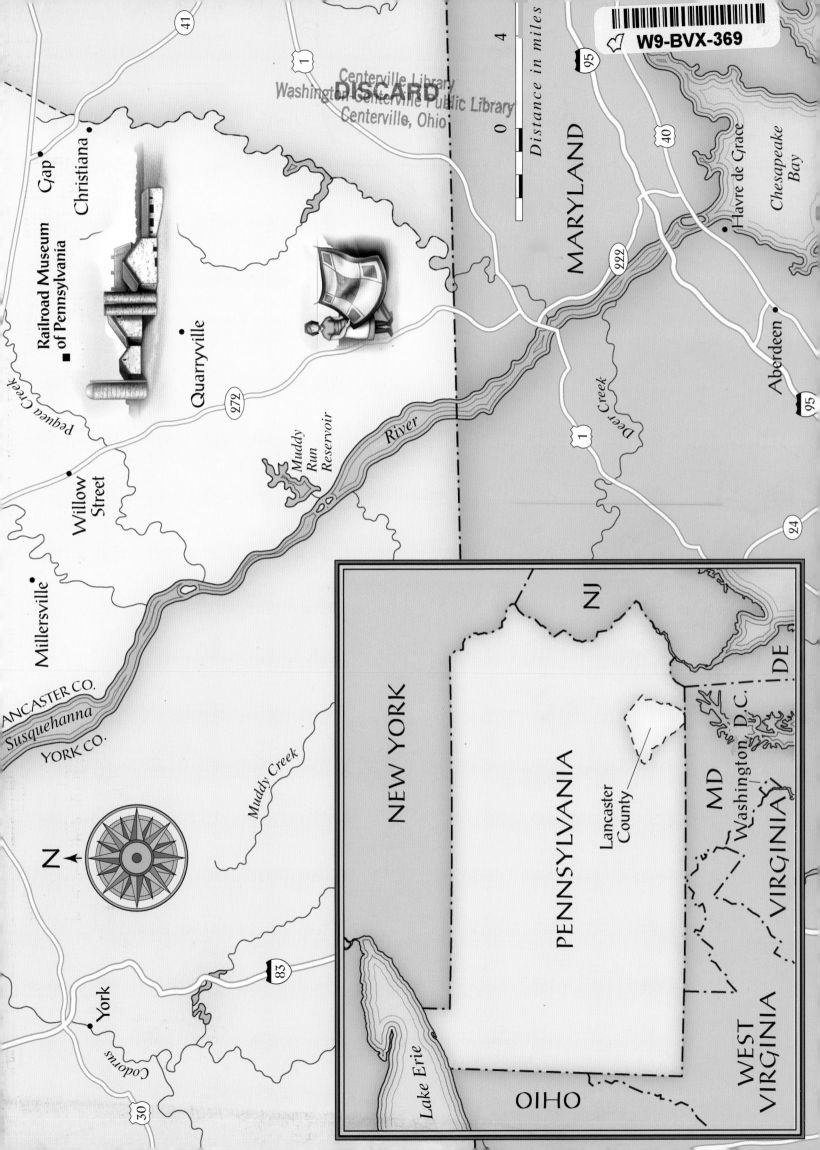

Distance in miles
0   4

41
1

Railroad Museum
of Pennsylvania ■

Gap •
Christiana •

Quarryville •

272

Willow
Street •

Millersville •

LANCASTER CO.
Susquehanna
YORK CO.

Pequea Creek

Muddy
Run
Reservoir

River

Muddy Creek

N

York •

Codorus

30

83

MARYLAND
95
40

222
1
Deer Creek

Havre de Grace •
Chesapeake
Bay

Aberdeen •
95
24

NEW YORK

NJ

PENNSYLVANIA

Lancaster
County

DE

MD
Washington, D.C.

VIRGINIA

WEST
VIRGINIA

OHIO

Lake Erie

CAROL M. HIGHSMITH AND TED LANDPHAIR

THE AMISH

A PHOTOGRAPHIC TOUR

CRESCENT BOOKS

NEW YORK

THE AUTHORS WISH TO THANK THE FOLLOWING FOR THEIR GENEROUS ASSISTANCE IN CONNECTION WITH THE COMPLETION OF THIS BOOK:

Mark Andrews, The Amish Farm & House, Lancaster, Pennsylvania
Robert W. McQuown, Mantua, Ohio
Joyce and Robert Mozenter, Philadelphia, Pennsylvania

———

This 1999 edition is published by Crescent Books®,
an imprint of Random House Value Publishing, Inc.,
201 East 50th Street, New York, N.Y. 10022.

Crescent Books and colophon are registered trademarks of
Random House Value Publishing, Inc.

Random House
New York • Toronto • London • Sydney • Auckland
http://www.randomhouse.com/

Printed and bound in China

Library of Congress Cataloging-in-Publication Data
Highsmith, Carol M., 1946–
The Amish / Carol M. Highsmith and Ted Landphair.
    p.   cm. — (A photographic tour)
      Includes index.
    ISBN 0-517-20398-7 (hc: alk. paper)
    1. Amish—United States—Pictorial works.
      2. Lancaster County (Pa.)—Tours.
    3. Lancaster County (Pa.)—Pictorial works.
 4. Amish—Pennsylvania—Lancaster County—Pictorial works.
      I. Landphair, Ted, 1942–   . II. Title.
 III. Series: Highsmith, Carol M., 1946–   Photographic tour.
  E184.M45H54   1999   98–35688
  974.8´150088287—dc21   CIP

8   7   6   5   4   3   2

———

Project Editor: Donna Lee Lurker

Designed by Robert L. Wiser, Archetype Press, Inc., Washington, D.C.

All photographs by Carol M. Highsmith unless otherwise credited:
map by XNR Productions, page 5; painting by P. Buckley Moss (permission to reproduce granted by P. Buckley Moss and the P. Buckley Moss Museum, Waynesboro, Virginia © 1998 P. Buckley Moss), page 6; Lancaster Mennonite Historical Society, pages 8–9; Free Library of Philadelphia, pages 10–21.

FRONT COVER: Calculating the horsepower of the classic Amish conveyance is a snap. Usually it's one. BACK COVER: Amish crafts, such as these rockers, are highly valued. PAGE 1: Amishmen wear straw hats most days, and black felt hats for religious services and special occasions. PAGES 2–3: Like those of a buggy, the wheels of Amish farm machinery are often made of wood and steel alone. The Amish believe that inflated rubber tires make it too tempting to stray from the community.

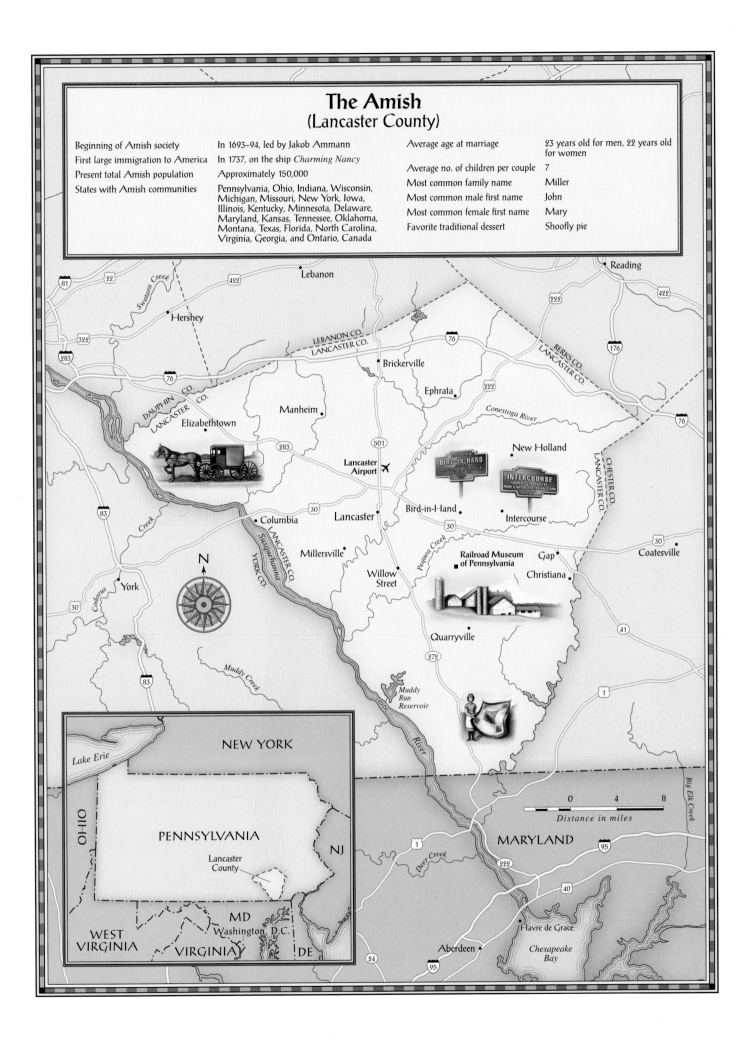

The Amish
(Lancaster County)

Beginning of Amish society	In 1693–94, led by Jakob Ammann	Average age at marriage	23 years old for men, 22 years old for women
First large immigration to America	In 1737, on the ship *Charming Nancy*	Average no. of children per couple	7
Present total Amish population	Approximately 150,000	Most common family name	Miller
States with Amish communities	Pennsylvania, Ohio, Indiana, Wisconsin, Michigan, Missouri, New York, Iowa, Illinois, Kentucky, Minnesota, Delaware, Maryland, Kansas, Tennessee, Oklahoma, Montana, Texas, Florida, North Carolina, Virginia, Georgia, and Ontario, Canada	Most common male first name	John
		Most common female first name	Mary
		Favorite traditional dessert	Shoofly pie

Distance in miles

THE OLD ORDER AMISH ARE THE MOST CONSPICUOUS Plain People. Their distinctive nineteenth-century lifestyle endures alongside the modern world at the cusp of the twenty-first century. They cheerfully acknowledge that they are living in a time warp as they drive horse-drawn buggies, open carts, and mule- or horse-pulled farm machinery. Their farms, located in the rural parts of twenty-two mostly eastern and midwestern U.S. states and eastern Canada, are often the largest, best kept, and most prosperous in their respective counties. Their homesteads are characterized by well-manicured gardens, windmills, and long rows of hanging wash on clotheslines, as well as the additions to their farmhouses that accommodate large extended families. What makes them especially easy to spot are the plain green window shades and, of course, the *absence* of electric wires, frilly curtains, or any other kind of other adornments.

However, the Amish are not separatists. They do not live in communes. Their handsome farms are spread alongside those of their non-Amish neighbors. The most noticeable difference is that their neighbor will plow his field with a motorized tractor, while the Amishman—or just as often, an Amish boy—will plow his with a team of draft horses or mules. (Some Old Order Amish outside Lancaster County, Pennsylvania, do not allow the use of mules because they were created by human cross-breeding of a donkey and a horse, and not by God.) Tobacco and cattle were once the Amish's chief cash crop. The manure from cattle fertilized the tobacco fields, and stockyards and gigantic tobacco warehouses stood on the outskirts of Lancaster and other eastern Pennsylvania towns. Today, dairy cattle, corn, and soybeans are the most prevalent cash crops.

While the Pennsylvania Amish community is second in size to that of eastern Ohio, which has the largest concentration of Amish, it is the richest. The demand for land in Lancaster County is so great that Amish farmers as well as non-Amish developers routinely bid against each other for available parcels. Since the Amish live simply and frugally, the wealthy among them do not spend their money on baubles, cruises, or fancy homes. They buy more land or put the money in the bank to save for future generations. The Amishmen need more land to meet their obligation to provide farms for their male offspring.

Amish congregations have been documented as far west as Montana and as far south as Texas. Their population in the United States is estimated to be near or above 150,000, with another 3,300 or more in eastern Canada. This number includes groups of New Order, or "Beachy," Amish—named for Amishman Moses Beachy from Somerset County, Pennsylvania, who led a walkout from an Amish community over the issue of shunning. Beachy Amish have incorporated some vestiges of modern technology into their lives. Sometimes called "Amish Mennonites," Beachy Amish even drive cars, albeit usually black ones with plain black bumpers. To further confuse visitors to "Amish country," members of some strict Mennonite orders drive buggies and reject modern technology in their homes, just as Old Order Amish do. To add to the array, there is a fourth group of humbly dressed Plain People in parts of Amish country as well. These are the "Dunkards"—German Baptists or "Brethren"—whose baptism ceremonies include immersion or "dunking."

The most famous and most-visited Amish settlement is in Lancaster County in eastern Pennsylvania, where the Old Order Amish, with their trademark gray buggies and plain clothes, live among the Mennonites (whose buggies here are black), the Brethren, as well as the "English." The Amish refer to people from outside their world as *Englishers,* and they and many Mennonites call themselves "Dutch."

Summer Wedding, P. Buckley Moss's oil painting, captures one of the biggest community events of the year: a nuptial ceremony conducted at the home of the bride. (Permission for use granted by P. Buckley Moss and the P. Buckley Moss Museum, Waynesboro, Virginia.)

Together, all the Plain People are often called "Pennsylvania Dutch," the English Quaker settlers' corruption of the word *deutsch*—the German language spoken by many immigrants to Pennsylvania. Old Order Amish are in fact trilingual: they speak High German at worship, English in school and in dealings with the "outside world," and a "Pennsylvania Dutch" German dialect—peppered with some words borrowed from English and softened by French influences from their time in Alsace—at home. In dealing with such matters as which cattle to buy or which saw blade to install, adult Amish will often mix English and Pennsylvania Dutch phrases.

Both the Mennonites—many of whom use electricity and drive automobiles, dress in modern clothes, and keep their children in school through high school and beyond—and the Amish are Anabaptists, who believe in adult baptism as a matter of free choice. The Anabaptist movement began in Switzerland in the early 1500s at the time of the Protestant Reformation. The name means "twice baptized," as their members—already baptized into the Roman Catholic Church as infants—were baptized a second time as adults. Later, Anabaptists rejected infant baptism, believing that the individual should make a free choice to accept a life with God. At that time, adult baptism was considered a criminal offense that was punishable by death, and many Anabaptists were imprisoned and tortured for their beliefs. Amish songs and books—like the *Martyrs Mirror*—keep stories of their persecution alive and contribute to ongoing Amish distrust of society at large. A favorite Amish story recalls the fate of Dutch Anabaptist Dirk Willems who pulled to safety a pursuing sheriff who had fallen through the ice on a pond; for his kindness, Willems was arrested and burned at the stake. And the reason Amishmen wear no mustaches dates to this period, for the soldiers who tormented them often wore long, florid mustaches.

To avoid detection, Anabaptists fled to the mountains or far-off rural regions, where many became farmers. In 1693, Anabaptists in the Alsace region—now part of France—broke away from the larger church. Jakob Ammann, their leader, believed that the Anabaptists had become too liberal in their lifestyle, straying from strict biblical teachings. Thereafter, Ammann's followers became known as the Amish, and Swiss Anabaptists as the Mennonites—a name derived from their leader, Menno Simons.

In the early 1700s, the Amish accepted the invitation of William Penn, Pennsylvania's founder, to Europeans of all religions to come to "Penn's Woods" and enjoy a life of freedom and religious tolerance. The Amish from Germany and Switzerland arrived in Philadelphia and, true to their history, promptly headed far into the wilderness in Bucks County and Lancaster County's Pequea River Valley, where the "world" could not follow. Such a notion seems preposterous today, as the "world" has built a jumble of outlet centers, strip shopping malls, and "Amish" attractions cheek to jowl with simple Amish farms. No Amish congregations remain in Europe.

There are no Amish church buildings, no religious icons other than the Bible (an edition originally translated into German by Martin Luther), no special Amish creed aside from following Christ's example by living simply and humbly and by helping others. Even personal Bible study is discouraged because it might lead to individual interpretations outside the accepted interpretation of God's word. The Amish believe that working the soil brings them close to God. Their worship is organized into

Anabaptists, fore-runners of the Amish and Mennonite sects, were exiled from the cities of Europe for their heretical belief in adult rather than infant baptism. Many Anabaptists later prospered in the remote countryside. This early-1800s woodcut shows a "new Anabaptist" sharpening his scythe.

LE
NOUVEL ANABAPTISTE,
ou
L'AGRICULTEUR-PRATIQUE.
N.º XXIV de la Collection.

Anabaptists were often ruthlessly persecuted for their beliefs. In the 1500s, many were tortured, beheaded, burned at the stake, or sent to the Mediterranean as galley slaves. Their stories inspired the lyrics of many Old German hymns that the Amish sing today.

districts of about twenty-five households led by a bishop. He and a permanent preacher are selected by lot after having been nominated by district members. Married men who, it is felt, will serve well in a leadership capacity are nominated, and those who receive three or more votes are finalists. A slip of paper is placed inside one Bible, and it and other Bibles are placed on a table and shuffled. Each finalist selects a Bible, and the one who chooses the one containing the paper is the new bishop, preacher, or deacon for life.

Services are held every *other* Sunday in each other's homes. Thus Old Order Amish are sometimes called "House Amish." In rooms cleared of household furniture, men and boys sit on one side, and women and girls on the other, and face a central area where leaders are seated. Beforehand, parishioners bring in long, backless wooden benches and dishware owned by the church district. Home worship harks back to the days in Europe when persecuted Anabaptists were forced to worship secretly. It reinforces the Amish belief that worship and daily life are inseparable; no fancy sanctuary or paid clergy is needed for communication with God.

The three-and-one-half-hour service begins with about thirty-five minutes of singing from the *Ausbund,* an 812-page German-language hymnal written by Anabaptists while they were imprisoned in Dassan Castle in the 1530s. There are no musical notes for the 140 songs in this hymnal, and no instruments accompany the singing, which is delivered slowly in a chant with no harmony. As many as sixty verses to favorite hymns are sung a cappella. The permanent preacher—who has no formal theological training—then delivers a short opening sermon that lasts fifteen minutes or so. Then comes a series of New Testament scriptures read from a booklet that lists twenty-six texts appropriate to the time of year. A second speaker—chosen by the congregation's leaders only moments before he begins speaking—then preaches the main sermon

In 1967, hundreds of visitors to Intercourse, Pennsylvania, looked into "Pennsylvania Dutch" homes during Summer Jubilee Weekend. These are Mennonite women—note the print dresses and simple jewelry, which Amish women would never wear. Approximately one hundred hours go into each quilt.

that lasts an hour or more, without notes of any kind. More scripture reading and comments (called "witnessing") from the congregation come next. Everyone then kneels for a prayer from a German prayer book, and then they stand for the benediction. There are two more matters remaining, however: announcements from the deacon and a closing hymn. Then women, who take no leadership role in any religious service, prepare a light, cold meal.

Offerings are collected only twice a year, at Eastertime and at fall communion services that can last seven hours or more. The service is followed by ritual foot-washing and the sharing of bread and wine, the latter made from grapes by the bishop's wife.

Religious holidays are solemn occasions. The Amish exchange small, practical gifts at Christmas, but there are no Christmas trees, lights, or Santa Claus figures to be found. Nor does Peter Cottontail hop down the bunny trail around Easter in Amish country.

Sunday afternoons are a time for play and socializing. Baseball and softball are passions among Amish youth, even though they do not listen to games on radio or watch them on television. Young singles—members of groups that the Amish call "gangs"—travel to other homes Sunday evenings for more hymn singing. A "date" will often consist of singing hymns or perhaps a spirited game of volleyball. It is to and from these events that a young Amishman will often drive a young Amish woman in an open "courting buggy"—a gift to the man from his father. A young man is usually presented with this courting buggy, costing up to $3,000, on his sixteenth birthday. An enclosed family buggy—sometimes laughingly called a "cheese box" in Amish country—costs about twice as much. Horses cost upwards of $2,500, and harnesses are as much as $1,000 more. Buggies, which must have lights (powered by batteries) and the familiar triangular rear reflectors, are sold at dealerships in communities with large Amish populations.

Amish elders often "look the other way" as many of their young people "sow their wild oats" and taste worldly pleasures for a period. In this time of modest rebellion, boys will wear fancy stovepipe hats or tilt the brims of their felt hats upwards in "cowboy fashion." It is not uncommon for Amish teenagers and young adults to obtain driver's licenses and drive cars, change from their traditional clothes into *Englisher* garb, and go dancing and bar-hopping. Even rock music blaring from radios in buggies can sometimes be heard. Young Amish have occasionally been arrested for drunken driving of buggies as well as automobiles. (Many more buggy drivers and passengers are the unfortunate victims of speeding automobiles or loco-motives, however.) Rascally behavior is tolerated because the young people have not yet joined the church. But once a young person accepts baptism—often at the time of marriage—all such worldly dalliances are forever banned. At baptism, the young Amishman or woman accepts the Christian faith and the authority of the group—spelled out in an unwritten *Ordnung,* or set of rules of behavior—for life.

Dating is a matter of free choice; there are no "arranged" Amish marriages. However, a young man must win the approval of not only his intended bride but also the area bishop. Courtship is never openly discussed until the bishop "publishes" the news of an upcoming wed-ding during announcements at a Sunday service. In anticipation of marriage, teenage Amish girls prepare a hope chest containing quilts and embroidery that they have completed as well as dishware and glasses they have received as birthday and Christmas presents.

Weddings are held in the bride's home on a Tuesday or Thursday, only in the fall after crops have been harvested and families can afford a day away from their fields. These are large, festive events with hundreds of guests and groaning boards of food. They are not, however, expensive affairs as there are no fancy wedding dresses, printed announcements, or wedding rings to buy; or florists, photog-raphers, or caterers to engage. There are no soloists or instrumental music, either. The new couple does not usually set up a household un-til the following spring. The bride and groom continue to work on their separate families' farms during the intervening winter, but they visit relatives and friends on weekends, receiving gifts as they go. This is the extent of an Amish honeymoon.

Marriage is encouraged but by no means expected. Unmarried Amishmen work farms or get jobs as carpenters, buggy makers, or mill employees. In areas of high Amish population such as Lancaster County, Amishmen are enthusiastic participants in volunteer fire departments, whose efforts, after all, often benefit Amish homes and farms. But the Amish do not participate in community or professional organizations, organized sports teams, or political parties. Since 1967, they have elected their own national steering committee in order to speak with a single voice on matters of national concern, such as how to respond to gov-ernment demands that they make worker's compensation payments. The Amish buy goods locally—especially raw materials, fertilizer, and farm machinery—from *Englisher* merchants and bank at town finan-cial institutions. And they often hold public auctions of farm equipment in February or March, prior to the planting season. Like weddings, these gatherings are prime social occasions for the community.

On a visit to New York in 1957, Amishman Noah Miller stopped to gaze at billboards touting the Broadway play "Plain and Fancy." Initially mistaken for a cast member, he was ushered inside. He saw the show from backstage and received an auto-graphed program.

Unmarried Amish women often leave home to run quilt, bake, or craft shops, or to work in Amish markets, tailor shops, or health-food stores; Lancaster County Amish women work as far away as Washington, D.C., Philadelphia, and cities in Delaware. Married Amish women also sometimes work outside the home as well, and two-income households are becoming almost as common among the Amish as in the community at large.

Obedience—children to parents and teachers, wives to husbands, and all to God's word—is central to the Amish way of life. So is glorification of God and the community, not the individual. Arrogance, pride, publicity, and adornments that call attention to oneself are forbidden. The Biblical admonition, "Pride cometh before the fall," is taught to Amish children.

It is therefore apt that Amish appearance and dress is plain and utilitarian. Amish girls and women wear their hair parted in the middle and pulled back in a bun; the hair is never cut. They wear prayer coverings at all times in public due to a biblical dictate that women shall keep their heads covered (1 Corinthians 11: "Every woman that prayeth or prophesieth with *her* head uncovered dishonoureth her head.... For a man indeed ought not to cover *his* head, forasmuch as he is the image and glory of God; but the woman is the glory of the man.... Neither was the man created for the woman; but the woman for the man"). Women's prayer coverings are usually white, but girls of marrying age will announce their availability by wearing black prayer coverings to religious services. When they travel, all Amish women and girls also wear bulky black bonnets, almost as big as hoods. Amish women's plain, long-sleeve dresses, which fall to ankle level, are pinned, as no buttons are allowed. Buttons are thought of as jewelry and are forbidden once a girl has been baptized. Even wedding rings are seen as too ostentatious. Girls wear a white half-apron until they are married, when they switch to a full, darker cape. The apron will be saved until a woman's death, and she will be buried in it. On cold days, a woman will wear a shawl and one or more sweaters, but never a coat.

Unmarried men are clean-shaven, and boys often are given bobbed "Dutch cut" haircuts. Married men grow beards, which, for the rest of their lives, they never trim. Men *do* wear buttons on their work clothes, but hooks and eyes only on formal "go-to-meetin'" outfits. They wear straw hats to keep the sun off their necks in warm weather and switch to black felt hats for worship and on cold days. Boys, from the moment they are potty-trained, wear the same clothes as men: straight-cut coats with no lapels and broadfall pants similar to sailor's pants with no zippers or belt loops—suspenders hold up the pants. White or colored shirts—always plain, never plaid or patterned—are worn to Sunday services and other special occasions. Shoes and socks worn by both sexes are plain black, though bishops in some Amish communities have allowed members to wear black running shoes. By comparison, even the most strict Mennonite sects allow their men and women to wear patterned shirts or dresses and shoes of all descriptions.

Work on an Amish farm is hard. "If you ever shook hands with an Amishman, you'd know," says Mark Andrews, manager of the Amish Farm & House in Lancaster. "His hands are very tough and callused, coarse and very strong. A very strong, firm hand." The Amish Farm & House is an authentic farmstead, no longer owned by the Amish but countenanced by them as a useful buffer to keep prying "guests," as

The Amish often pitch in to help their neighbors—Amish and otherwise. Amishman Chris Kauffman carries a cinder block for a chimney on the new second floor of non-Amishman Bob Barnett of Parksburg, Pennsylvania, who had recently married and needed more room.

they call tourists, from intruding too deeply onto their farms and lives. The property's original stone house was built by Quakers in 1805 and occupied by Old Order Amish for a time. As in many Amish farm homes, an addition was built to house retiring grandparents, who could thus retain separate lives and respect the privacy of the younger family. However, these *Dawdy Haus,* or "Grandfather House," additions are always connected to the main house, so no additional real-estate taxes can be assessed.

The farms in Pennsylvania Dutch country in the rural eastern section of the Keystone State are known for the colorful hex signs that adorn several barns, but these are not the work of Amish or Mennonite farmers. Hex signs were brought to the area from the Rhineland in the early 1700s as good-luck symbols to ward off evil spirits. They are now strictly decorative items on some *Englisher* barns.

Amish homes are generally devoid of decoration, although they will hang calendars, photographs of scenery, dried flowers, and family records listing the birthdate of each person. Pillows, quilts, and rugs, however, are often vividly colored. The kitchen is usually the largest and busiest room in an Amish house. The centerpiece is the family table, often an "eight-board" variety to accommodate the large family. Often the kitchen is the only heated room, and the sick are often tended to there. Some are bright and modern-looking, equipped with appliances such as refrigerators and washing machines run by propane gas. But one will not find dishwashers, toasters, microwave ovens, or, indeed, electric outlets there. Most Amish homes have no deep freezers, though expensive gas-powered models have been developed. Amish get around this problem by bartering produce in exchange for freezer space at a non-Amish neighbor's farm.

"Barn raisings" are a traditional Amish custom in which friends come from far and near to work, often for days, in building or rebuilding structures. Wives prepare hearty meals. As usual, work is done by hand with no help from electricity.

True to their German tradition, Amish women prepare filling meals rich in fat and protein. Breakfast usually includes eggs, fried potatoes, cornmeal mush, and sausage or bacon, plus—especially in Pennsylvania—sweet and sticky shoofly pie. The midday meal is the day's largest. It often features beef or chicken soups or pot pies, mashed potatoes and gravy, an assortment of vegetables and German noodles, sauerkraut, homemade root beer, and pies. Meals at the end of the day, after sunset and only a short time before bedtime, are usually quick and light.

Women tend to their large gardens, freeze and can fruits and vegetables, and sew using treadle-powered machines. At mealtime, men and boys are always served first, followed by the women and girls. At meals associated with religious services, the bishop, deacon, and preacher are the first to be served.

The Amish do not evangelize or proselytize as they believe that their works and faith speak for themselves. They welcome converts but few *Englishers,* who find it difficult to renounce modern conveniences, make the transition. One Amish woman reports that potential converts find it even harder to give up their automobiles than to do without television, radio, computers, or other electronic devices. "Mobility, the freedom to travel far and wide, is a terrible temptation," she says. To grow—and the Amish in America have grown from a few hundred families in 1900—the sect relies on simple procreation; they do not practice birth control. Amish families of seven, eight, or as many as fifteen children are not unusual, and they often share bedrooms with as many as three or four siblings of the same sex. Offspring are needed, of course, to support large Amish farms, though prosperous farmers will also employ non-Amish labor, especially during the harvest season.

The Amish also work outside the farm in cottage industries from broom-making to the construction of wooden storage sheds, gazebos, and toys. Older boys sometimes hire out as carpenters, and girls as housekeepers. Their wages go to their parents until they reach eighteen, at which point they may keep half as a nest-egg for marriage. Factory labor is not permitted because it is believed that this kind of work would take fathers from their families for too many hours, and corporate benefits like pension plans would lessen the dependence upon the Amish community.

The Amish may be modest in other realms, but they are ambitious in business. Common at the end of an Amish family's driveway are tiny, hand-printed signs announcing "bunnies for sale" or simply "quilts—no Sunday sales." No other signs, billboards, or advertisements will be found. Like *Englishers,* the Amish take advantage of tourism; they want strangers to come, see, and buy, but not pry. The Amish grow weary of gawkers and trespassers. "Yes, we're different," they say. "But you're different, too. Why do we dress the way we do? We would turn around and say, 'Why do *you* dress the way you do?'"

The Amish vote in local elections, but usually not in state or national contests. Because of their opposition to the use of violence, Amishmen will not serve in the military services; in wartime, they have traditionally been exempted from service as conscientious objectors and given noncombat roles. (Some Amish do, however, keep rifles for hunting and share hunting cabins in the Pennsylvania mountains.)

Thus the Amish are often called the Gentle People, and this meek spirit extends to civilian life as well. The Amish will not bring lawsuits against others, for instance, and their rejection of government-ordered zoning regulations, building codes, and even use of hard hats on construction sites has sometimes landed them to jail. Their passivity can be traced to the Amish *Gelassenheit*—belief in what historian Donald Kraybill calls "self-surrender, resignation to God's will, yielding to others, self-denial, contentment, and a quiet spirit." In other words, humility, modesty, and reserve.

Yet they are aggressive in applying the extreme measure of shunning to those who, once baptized, leave the fold or flout the *Ordnung.* Not only is the miscreant excommunicated—a common practice in many religions—he or she is also socially ostracized by the group, including one's own parents and siblings. The person may remain with his or her Amish spouse, but sexual relations are forbidden until and unless the person renounces the wicked behavior and returns to the fold. Many who *do* leave Amish life gravitate toward Mennonite and other strict, though technologically more progressive, congregations.

While English is spoken in school and in dealings with the outside world, Pennsylvania German is the language of Amish homes and religious services. Maintaining a separate language helps insulate and perpetuate the community. Donald Kraybill, whose written portrait of the Amish appears in the *Gale Encyclopedia of Multicultural America,* has estimated that four of five Amish children stay in the fold by accepting adult baptism and formally joining the Amish church. The Amish do not look unfavorably upon young people who leave because they have not yet been baptized and accepted into the church. Parents know that the temptations to *stay* are as strong as the allure of the world at large. Within the community there is love, support,

Soft pretzels— with a side of yellow mustard—are grabbed up hot and fresh out of the oven at the Pennsylvania Dutch Festival at the Reading Terminal Market in Philadelphia. The market is one of the favorite outlets for Amish food and crafts.

Horse shows, sales, and auctions are regular events, vital to the economy of Amish country. They are not all business, however. Folks of all ages come just to admire the animals. Of course, some views are better than others.

and security; outside there is uncertainty, loneliness, and unknown expectations. In *The Gentle People,* James A. Warner and Donald M. Denlinger describe an ambitious young Amishman who leaves the community to join the Air Force. An honorable discharge casts him back into civilian life.

His memories of a childhood sweetheart haunted him till he returned to see what became of her. She was still a maidal (unmarried), but still of the old order Amish, which forbade his trespassing on her farm. However, outside rendezvous soon rekindled their love. They went to the Bishop, confessed and repented to the church which received them back. The lad is now an old order Amishman who went from supersonic jet speeds back to the slow pace of the horse and buggy.

To conform with federal and state laws, Amish children attend school until they reach age fifteen, at which time they leave to help full-time on the farm or at home. Usually schooling ends with the completion of the eighth grade, but if an Amish child has completed that grade but is not yet fifteen, he or she will stay in school for three hours a week until the fifteenth birthday.

Amish children may attend public school, but more common in heavily Amish areas are one-room, English-language Amish parochial schools, where, as in worship, girls sit on one side of a central aisle, boys on the other. Many one-room schools are still heated by a single iron stove into which the teacher shovels coal. In 1972, the U.S. Supreme Court upheld the right of the Amish to operate these schools independent of the public system. The Amish school curriculum reinforces religion. One set of schoolroom guidelines reads:

> In Arithmetic by accuracy (no cheating).
> In English by learning to say what we mean.
> In History by humanity (kindness-Mercy).
> In Geography by learning to make a [sic] honest living from the soil.
> In Music by singing praises to God.

Is Religion then continuously mentioned? Seldom, just enough to bring the whole thing to a point now and then.

> *The Goal Of The Old Order Amish Parochial Schools*
> *Is To Prepare For Usefulness, By Preparing For Eternity.*

The teacher in an Amish school is usually a young, single girl who herself has completed only the eight grades. The number of school days just meets the minimum required by law so the children can work the most days possible at home or in the fields. There is rarely homework, again because completing it would cut into work time. (Amish children go to bed early and with little protest, knowing they will be up at five to help with chores.) In 1992, a teacher in a small Lancaster County school told an interviewer that her students were not permitted to whisper or leave their seats. Discipline, including paddling for those who repeat disruptive behavior, she said, was administered after school. James Warner and Donald Denlinger call this the "Amish board of education on their seat of learning." Students are assigned chores in school, and games include Kick the Can, Fox and Geese, Jump Rope, Hopscotch, baseball, and a form of baseball called "Roundtown" that employs four batters, with everyone else positioned in the outfield. (Fun is also homemade on the farm, where pets and handmade toys, chess and checkers, sleds or roller skates, plus baseballs and bats, easily fill the few hours available for idle play.)

The Amish pay income and sales taxes but not Social Security tax; they have no need for Social Security benefits as their sick and elderly are cared for at home. They will also pool financial resources to help an individual or family who has suffered a setback, and Amish barn-raisings for families—Amish and *Englisher* alike—whose barns have burned are a community tradition. They treat illnesses with old-time remedies where possible, but the Amish have no aversion to modern medical or dental treatment—or veterinarian services for their animals—when it is called for. They carry no medical insurance, however, so to hold the line on medical expenses they will often visit chiropractors, clinics, or osteopaths rather than medical doctors or hospitals when possible. Firstborns are usually delivered in a hospital setting, but additional babies are usually delivered at home with a midwife's help.

"When it comes to technology, the Amish aren't really close-minded, just choosy," writes Eric Brende in a 1996 *Technology Review* article. He cites their inventiveness in developing such devices as a cookstove with an airtight combustion compartment, a John Deere tractor refitted for hay baling, and even an aerodynamic scythe that requires little stooping. "A glance at their efforts reveals beautiful, well-maintained farms thriving in an age when many others cannot even survive," Brende observes. Amish farm equipment must have only steel or wooden wheels, for the same reason that the Amish allow tricycles, roller skates, and push scooters but

When the officials of Leacock Township, Pennsylvania, proposed subdividing a local farm into one hundred housing plots in 1990, Amishmen joined in a protest. The Amish, looking to expand their prosperous farms, often vie with developers seeking to build homes and shopping centers.

Amish kids pour from a one-room schoolhouse at recess time in Bareville, in Lancaster County's Pennsylvania Dutch country. When this photograph was taken in 1961, there were about one hundred such schools, serving students ages five to fourteen, operating in Pennsylvania.

not bicycles: rubber wheels on vehicles would make travel away from the community and into the temptations of the world at large too easy. It goes without saying, then, that Old Order Amish may not own cars. However, they may ride in automobiles when necessary, as in medical emergencies, and "English" taxi services do good business in heavily Amish communities. Likewise, the Amish will hire a driver to visit far-off relatives, and Amish businesses often employ non-Amish workers who own cars, vans, and trucks in order to move people and products as needed. Without them, there could be no fresh meat and produce at Amish markets located on the fringes of big cities far from the farm. Train and intercity bus travel is permitted, but air travel is almost never allowed.

The Amish eschew the use of 110-volt electricity, not so much because it represents modern convenience, but because electric service provided by a local or regional company represents a tangible tie to the outside world that the Amish wish to avoid. The same proscription applies to natural gas supplied from pipelines, though the Amish will power their stoves, washing machines, lights, and power tools by propane and kerosene (which they control), hydraulics, or compressed air. Electricity from individual twelve-volt batteries is also acceptable. Shop tools are run by power generated from a line shaft connected to a gasoline or diesel engine, or by pneumatic pressure from large tanks filled with compressed air. Diesel and gasoline engines are permitted as emergency back-ups to water-powered pumps, and the Amish will use small engines to run their milking machines, coolers, hay balers, and corn pickers. The Amish were forced by milk distributors to install bulk, refrigerated milk tanks, but these are cooled by diesel engines rather than outside electricity. Some Amish even permit the use of powerful diesel tractors—with steel wheels only—in and around the barn and farmstead. Their motors power such machinery as grinders and ventilating fans. In a compromise that is often baffling to non-Amish onlookers, Amish farmers will employ a tractor to cut and bind grass and wheat, but it cannot be driven. It must be pulled from place to place by a team of horses or mules.

Modern plumbing was readily accepted by the Amish, and many bishops allowed telephones in Amish homes when the devices were first introduced. But after people were found to be gossiping, spending valuable work time on the phone and visiting each other less, the telephones were ordered removed. Pay phones can now be found at the end of country lanes on some Amish farms, and there is no prohibition against their use. One will not find Amish families listed in telephone directories, however.

The Amish may use battery-powered calculators but not computers, a distinction that Donald Kraybill, in his booklet *The Puzzles of Amish Life,* calls one of the "practical, cultural compromises—bargains that the Amish have struck between traditional ways and the powerful forces of modernization." The Amish are willing to change, Kraybill writes, "but not at the expense of communal values and ethnic identity. They are willing to use modern technology, but not when it disrupts family and community stability." Amish accommodation with change, in short, amounts to "selective modernization." Still, Kraybill writes, "Church leaders view themselves as 'watchmen on the wall of Zion,' on the lookout for little foxes of worldliness that might undermine the spiritual and social welfare of the community."

The Amish's different ways are a source of endless fascination to visitors. The Amish themselves are accustomed to being stared or pointed at, and they do grow weary of it. Lancaster County in Pennsylvania, Holmes County in Ohio, or St. Mary's County in Maryland is not Colonial Williamsburg; the Amish people whom visitors come to see are not actors or "historic interpreters." "That's why it's our job to explain exactly how they live and why they do the things they do," says Mark Andrews of the Amish Farm & House. "We show our guests some of the things they should *not* be doing so that they can respect Amish culture. One of those things is taking pictures of them, which offends them very much." Following the Biblical commandment, "Thou shalt not make to thyself a graven image, nor the likeness of anything that is in heaven or in the earth beneath," the Amish consider statues and photographs of faces to be vain and prideful, too boastful to fit into their humble, group-oriented culture. Even their dolls have no faces. "While other Americans work hard to 'find themselves,'" writes Donald Kraybill, "Amish work hard to 'lose themselves' in the goals and activities of their communities."

The Amish read local magazines and newspapers but avoid splashy national publications. Many throughout the United States and Canada, however, do read the national edition of *The Budget,* a newspaper published in Sugarcreek, a town of two thousand in the heart of Ohio's Amish country. This newspaper is, in fact, one of the few institutions outside the Amish fold that has helped hold the far-flung community together. In addition to the usual small-town news of eastern Ohio, *The Budget* has

Like other school-children, Amish kids occasionally get to enjoy the simple pleasures of a field trip. These youngsters wait beside a window of a water tank at the Philadelphia Zoo, hoping to come nose to nose with a swimming polar bear.

for more than a century published letters from Amish and Mennonite readers from Texas to Ontario. The paper prints many homespun, mundane anecdotes of family life and travels, and often includes long lists of people attending weddings, community suppers, and the like.

Three examples from *The Budget* that validate the Amish kinship with the land:

(From Amelia, Virginia) Leroy Lehman had a distressing day of work on Sunday, when his silo unloader wouldn't work, and the cows needed to be fed. He was able to get needed equipment from an old unused silo on Floyd Mast's place, but it was time consuming.

(From Prairie Home, Missouri) Showers every few days. Leaves are coming on the trees. We had our first asparagus a week ago, but is still growing slow. Rhubarb ready to use.

(From Hillsboro, Wisconsin) Our boys were determined to find a few mushrooms in March yet, if everything else is a month early, but that is now ruled out. The spring peepers are really enjoying this weather, their first outing, and during the day the chirping sparrows' song fills the air.

The Amish often tolerate a brief "sowing of wild oats" by unmarried youths. This Lancaster Amishman told the Philadelphia Evening Bulletin *that he drove a car as well as worked in a factory, in defiance of Amish custom.*

Smaller, more localized competitors of *The Budget* have grown up in some communities that have a heavy Amish population. To attract readers, they tout their limited use of display advertising (yet another worldly temptation). Amish businesses rarely advertise. About as dramatic a notice as one will find is a placard on the front door of a hardware store in eastern Ohio's Amish country. It noted that another branch of the store could be found a few miles distant in another town, "just eight minutes by car, twenty-two minutes by buggy."

Because of their healthy lifestyles, Amish people often live into their eighties and nineties, as a walk through a simple Amish cemetery will attest. These graveyards, in open fields, are usually surrounded by white fences. Tombstones are simple, and none rise ostentatiously above any other. Many will list not just the deceased's dates of birth and death, but also the exact number of years, months, and days that the person lived on earth. When an Amish person dies, the body is taken to an *Englisher* mortician for embalming. It is then returned home where family members (usu-

ally the deceased's children, who consider it the last thing they can do in appreciation of a parent's love) dress the body in white and place it in a simple six-sided, European-style wooden coffin. Viewing and a religious service follow in the home. A horse-drawn hearse then leads a procession of buggies to the cemetery for burial.

The honest, hardworking Amish make tidy neighbors and are a growing tourist curiosity, but they are not universally admired. Critics call them backward and even selfish, arguing that they take advantage of some of modern society's benefits, such as advances in agriculture, science, and veterinary medicine, but put little back into the community at large. They do not send their children to college or into the world, support the armed services, participate in most elections, or join philanthropic and community-service organizations. Their horses, buggies, and wagons tear up asphalt roads, but they pay no gasoline taxes to repair them. The Amish reply, quite simply, that they pay millions of dollars in other taxes but use far fewer public services than other groups. And where the Amish live in great numbers, communities are cleaner, safer, less wasteful, more peaceful, and less cluttered than other towns down the road.

Crashes involving automobiles and buggies are all too common. In this one, a forty-four-year-old Amishman was killed, and his horse had to be destroyed. A car whose driver claimed his brakes failed slammed into them near Intercourse, Pennsylvania.

Although the Amish are not the only tourist attraction in places like Lancaster County, Pennsylvania, and Tuscarawus County, Ohio, they help bring millions of tourists and hundreds of millions of dollars into these communities annually. Indeed, while "Dutch" and "Pennsylvania Dutch" attractions—including pretzel factories, quilts, curios, antiques, and smorgasbords and other family-style restaurants—are marketed by tourism officials in these areas, it is the Amish whom visitors come to see. Little wonder names like "Amishland," "Amish Village," "Premium Natural Amish Cheese," "Amish Country Peddler," and "Amish-style" appear almost as frequently as references to the "Dutch" in these parts. Visitors to Lancaster County delight in the distinctive names of many of its towns, such as Bird-in-Hand, named in 1764 for an inn where two road surveyors decided to stop, one citing the adage, "A bird in hand is worth two in the bush." Another is Blue Ball, originally a Native American village called "Blue Google," meaning gurgling or running waters. In 1776 a hotel was built in town, and its sign was a large copper ball painted blue. The most famous Lancaster County town of all is Intercourse, located at the intersection, or intercourse, of two famous old highways—King's Highway and Newport Road.

Amish life is quaint but by no means idyllic. These are plain, not perfect, people, and very much a people apart. They cling stubbornly to old ways, resist new ones, and keep to themselves. They occasionally feud among themselves. Births out of wedlock, mental illness, family violence, and suicide are not unknown in their midst. But the Amish are also by all accounts loving and supportive parents. Their houses are homes—safe and inviting for old and young. The "information age" passes the Amish by, but so do the temptations and stresses that grip the outside world. The Amish can and do fairly ask of their worldly neighbors, "Where is all your 'progress' taking you? Are you happier? More loved? More fulfilled?" Seen in this light, the wholesome life of North America's Plain People does not seem so "backward" at all.

OVERLEAF: Amish farms are classic in their simple beauty. No electric or telephone wires or poles clutter the scene. Elderly grandparents usually live in additions built onto the main farmhouse of a large Amish family. There are no Amish retirement communities, and the Amish are exempted from paying Social Security taxes because the community cares for elders at home.

Every square foot of good land, on hill-sides as well as level ground, is tilled on an Amish farm (above). Implements (opposite) are crude by modern standards, but effective. At first glance from a nearby road, this man (overleaf) looks like another hard-working Amishman. But there are clear clues that he is a Mennonite. His hat lacks the telltale wide brim, and note the rubber balloon tires on his wagon.

It is Amish tradition to paint some of the trees along narrow paths (opposite) as a safety measure. Painted trunks are easy to see—and avoid—in tight quarters. The entire Amish family's work is never done. Here, a boy helps his dad work a mule near the barn (above). The soil of Lancaster County (overleaf) is some of the richest in America. The Amish say they feel close to God when they work the land.

Depending upon the job, teams of six horses (top right)— or even more horses or mules—are a common sight on Amish farms. Sometimes girls and women pitch in (bottom right) behind the plow or on a big hay wagon. The windmill (opposite) is a trademark of an Amish farm. It pulls water for the family and farm animals. Boys get a taste of dusty, grueling work behind a team at an early age (overleaf).

Amish farms (opposite) are usually the most prosperous in the area. Though they lack "modern conveniences," their structures are built to last. One is hard-pressed to find a dilapidated barn on Amish property. Raising dairy cattle (above) is lucrative, and rich milk, cream, cheese, and other dairy products are significant cash crops and a staple at stores in the area and farmers' markets on the outskirts of big cities.

Biblical parables direct the Amish to be stewards of the soil. Though their equipment (left) is humble, their skills at crop rotation—learned over centuries in Europe—and careful farm management have helped them succeed. It does not hurt that the Amish have secured some of the most fertile land on earth in Pennsylvania and nearby states. Every plow, tool, and tub (above) on the Amish farm is practical and effective.

A bountiful crop starts with plain sacks of seed (above). Tobacco (opposite), once a leading cash crop in Amish country, has declined in importance, in part because urbanization has gobbled up prime tobacco farmland. Amish farms (overleaf) are never ostentatious —there are no curlicues, paintings, or "hex signs" to be found— but there is nothing in Amish tradition that says a family cannot paint its barn roofs a dazzling red.

The Amish make ingenious use of motors (opposite), which, in the absence of outside electrical service, power everything from machinery around a barn to milk chillers inside. Work on a hay baler (top and bottom left) involves plenty of both machine and muscle power, with an emphasis on the latter. There is no more important crop than hay because it sustains farm animals through the cold winter in the states where the Amish thrive.

It takes a combination of human, horse, and mule power (top right) to get a tough job done on an Amish farm. There are no giant combines or air-conditioned cabs. Teamwork (bottom right) is stressed. Everybody in the family pitches in (opposite), for there is no wasted time or space. Except for a hand with heavy spading to prepare the ground, gardening and weeding are almost exclusively women's and children's work.

Truck crops like these cabbages (above) make their way into soups, sauerkraut, and salads. Fruit and produce are canned for the winter at home. Still more is prepared for sale in farmers' markets. You will not see too many roadside stands in Amish country as they involve too much idle time waiting for customers. In some parts of Pennsylvania, Ohio, Indiana, and other eastern and midwestern states, clusters of tidy Amish farms (right) dominate the landscape.

Do chickens (above) or eggs come first to an Amish market? They are brought together, and both usually sell quickly. So do chicks, rabbits, ducklings, canned vegetables and fruit, and crafts of all descriptions. Clever pragmatism can be seen in just about everything the Amish touch. Note the simplicity and effective air flow of this inventive corn crib (opposite). Green corn is often chopped near the barn and blown into larger silos (overleaf).

You will not find corncobs— or anything else— strewn around an Amish farmstead. They are neatly and carefully stored (opposite). An Amishman or woman could easily have written the old maxim: "A place for everything, and everything in its place." At Amish lumber mills even sawdust (above) is neatly conserved for use in making fiberboard.

At first glance, the
equipment being
rolled down a country
road by this Amish-
man (right) looks
highly mechanized.
But note the steel
wheels, which limit
its mobility. As usual,
it is pulled by horses,

not a tractor, and it
is powered by a small
gasoline generator.
The Amish are superb
dairy producers.
They watch over their
herds carefully, and
occasionally the
cows keep an eye on
them as well (above).

There is simple
beauty all around
you in Amish
country. This big
wheel (opposite) is
leaning against a
fence at the Amish
Farm & House in
Lancaster. You will
not see these caution
signs (above) in
many places outside
Amish country.
They are a warning
to automobile drivers
that they may
suddenly encounter a
slow-moving horse
and buggy as well as
that the Amish and
Mennonite rigs will
be crossing at inter-
sections and slowly
pulling out into
traffic. A cluster of
buggies (overleaf) is a
good sign it is Sunday
"visiting time"
after a full day's reli-
gious service.

Buggy drivers keep not just to the right, but usually the far right (opposite), to allow automobiles to pass. The Amish rarely "catch a lift" down the road. They walk (top left) and carry bulky articles between them as needed. While the Amish do not allow full-sized bicycles— they bring too much freedom and mobility—this little model (bottom left) is more of a scooter. Sometimes enough buggies come together (overleaf) to make a "parking lot"!

The Amish would likely not allow even this small amount of peeling paint (left) on their farmstead; this horse and wagon were hitched in town on market day. Home is the center of Amish family life, but families also travel together whenever possible (above). On alternate Sundays, with few chores to be done, the Amish ride to each other's homes for religious services; the intervening Sundays are free for visiting and games.

The horses have been let out to pasture, and the buggies lined up "for a spell" (opposite) as families come together for Sunday services. Just as the "English" have automobile dealerships and used-car lots, so the Amish line up carriages for sale (top left). Buggy dealerships and blacksmith shops are tourist attractions. Sometimes a buggy will have space for groceries or other cargo, like a horse-drawn "sport utility vehicle" (bottom left).

A surprising number of adults and kids can squeeze into an Amish buggy (opposite). Grown-ups will usually pass strangers without much of a nod, but children (above) often cannot resist playful peeks, waves, and making silly faces. Herr's Mill Bridge near Stras-burg (overleaf), one of twenty-eight covered bridges in Lancaster County, is a national historic landmark and a photographer's delight. Just behind it is the seventeenth-century Mill Bridge Village.

Two boys (top right) hide their faces from a photographer because the Amish consider posing to be vain. Few scenes seem to turn back the clock as vividly as an Amish open buggy passing through an old Lancaster County covered bridge (bottom right). The Amish may be loath to show off themselves or their way of life, but others are quick to exploit the appeal of Amish images and symbols (opposite).

Amish country is full of craft stores that feature skilled carpentry products. Farm animals (above) are a favorite theme of woodworking craftsmen. The Old Village Store in Bird-in-Hand (opposite) makes good use of popular "hex signs." Use of such signs to ward off evil spirits is an old German tradition—but not an Amish one. You will not find the signs, which are now purely decorative, on Amish barns or houses.

Intercourse, Pennsylvania (top right), got its provocative name from a tame, old-fashioned word for intersection. The town developed at an important local crossroads. The story of Bird-in-Hand (bottom right) involves the familiar adage that somebody applied to a swinging sign depicting a bird on the town hotel. The name "Gap" (opposite) has purely geographical roots. Also in Lancaster County are Blue Ball, Compass, Ronks, Smoketown, and Buck.

Many advertising signs (left) make clever use of everyday Amish scenes. The Amish themselves keep promotions of their home-based businesses to a minimum. The porcine weathervane (above) twirls above a turret on the big farmers' market building in Bird-in-Hand, Pennsylvania.

One way to tell an Amish farm without looking down the road is to watch for "Closed Sunday" signs, or, in this case (above), a notice posted at Eastertide that business would not be conducted on the holiest of weekends. Sunday is a day of rest, devoid of commerce, in Amish country. Amish craftsmen produce some of the sturdiest, most creative, and most useful handicrafts (opposite) in the nation. Among them, an array of well constructed birdhouses (overleaf). The buyer knows that no shortcuts were used to make Amish crafts.

Wilkom

Zook's Dutch Novelties ©1996

This colorful placard (opposite) borrows from the tradition of hex signs. The Amish might make such a sign at their craft shops, but they themselves would never display such an ostentatious symbol. In Ohio, Amish goods are the draw at a flea market (top left). Like other unusually named towns in Pennsylvania Dutch country—such as Intercourse and Blue Ball—Gap (bottom left) features a variety of antique and Amish craft stores. And "Amish" souvenir options (overleaf) are plentiful. Words like "Dutch Country" and silhouettes of men with hats and beards are used to suggest an Amish tie that is not always there.

Whoopie pies (above) are another Amish taste treat. They are not pies but soft chocolate, vanilla, or oatmeal cakes overstuffed with creamy filling. At Philadelphia's Reading Terminal Market, an Amish girl (right) serves a batch of soft pretzels. There and at Amish markets from suburban Washington, D.C., to cities in Ohio, Amish pastries, meats, cheeses, ice cream, vegetables, and salads are big sellers. Most markets have sit-down cafés for short-order meals as well.

The Amish bake an infinite variety of breads, cookies, pies, strudels, and donuts. But you won't find many overweight Amish; they work off excess calories. Shoofly pies (opposite), made from gooey molasses-based filling and sometimes topped with chocolate cream, get their colorful name for obvious reasons. The pie mix is a popular souvenir, and some retailers (above)— borrowing once again from the "Dutch" symbolism—tout the fattening treats.

This giant of an Amishman (above) greets visitors across the street from the Pennsylvania Dutch Visitors Bureau welcome center off U.S. Route 30 in Lancaster. The center offers Amish country maps, books, an orientation film, and keepsakes. Some of the big attractions lie along Route 30, but smaller shops selling items like these mailboxes (opposite) are found along U.S. 340 to Bird-in-Hand and Intercourse. Beautiful Amish farms surround both highways. At Millcreek Market, an Amish craftsman (overleaf) checks his unpainted dollhouses, swings, and desks. Customers know that every Amish piece is made by hand, and made to last. Don't look for many sales or discounts, however; Amish merchants set a fair price and usually stick to it.

OLS
BOY
SWINGR

Amish figures (left) swing in the wind outside an embroidery shop in Intercourse, and other wooden cutouts (above) are displayed near a Bird-in-Hand crafts store. Genuine Amish dolls, such as those (overleaf) from Sugar-creek, Ohio, have one distinction that ensures an Amish family might buy one for their children: the dolls have no facial features. It is another example of the Amish prohibition against displaying "graven images."

The Amish do not allow much decoration in their homes, so their beautiful quilts (above) immediately catch the eye. At Lancaster's Amish Farm & House, a boy's ordinary straw hat and his "go-to-meetin'" felt hat lie side by side on his bed (opposite). Many dolls and clothes are made on treadle-powered sewing machines (overleaf) in Amish homes. This one is displayed at the Amish Farm & House in Lancaster.

Another sure sign of an Amish farm is a clothesline (above and opposite) straining under the weight of the large family's clothes and quilts. Monday is usually washday, and neither electric nor gas washers and dryers do the job. The Amish decline such services not so much because of their convenience, but because utility luxuries originate in the community at large and would tie the Amish world inextricably to the outside world. The cotton quilts hanging on a line (overleaf) at Hannah's Quilts in Lancaster are designed as artistic wall hangings, not for use on a bed. They are not inexpensive.

Amish women's
dresses (left), hanging
here at the Amish
Farm & House in
Lancaster, fall to the
ankles. They are
always plain, with no
patterns or buttons.
On cool days, older
girls and women
bundle up in dark
sweaters. Their
heads are covered
at all times in public
(above). An Amish
couple's master
bedroom (overleaf)
is simple. As in all
rooms in the house,
plain green shades,
never frilly curtains,
keep out the light.

Classic one-room schoolhouses like this one (left) can still be found in Amish country. Amish children stay in school through the eighth grade. Then they go to work full-time at home. Even though chores await school-children after classes, it is a relief when the school day is over (above). Teachers in the independent Amish schools typically assign little homework, knowing their students will be in bed early and up early the next day.

Like kids anywhere, Amish schoolchildren trade goodies from their lunchboxes (above). You will rarely see an Amish child with a lunch pail adorned with cartoon superheroes since the children do not watch television. At home, the kitchen (opposite) is the undisputed center of the household. This is the one place where the entire family can share prayers, stories, and plans. Except on special occasions, only the women of the household cook and bake.

Home-canned goods (opposite) are a taste treat, carefully "put up" in season for use in other seasons. The kitchen fills with wonderful fragrances, and sampling is irresistible. They are enjoyed not just in Amish homes but also by shoppers at area farmers' markets. Softball and baseball are favorite Amish sports, both in school and in the limited play time at home (above). Boys and girls play the game, and variations, together.

Free time is precious to all members of an Amish family. Among the most leisured moments are alternate Sundays when religious services are not held. This little girl (above) is making up a simple game. It involves tossing clods of dirt toward a pot not far away. Like any farm family, Amish people keep pets as well as barnyard animals. Goats (opposite) can be both; their milk makes delicious—and salable—cheese.

The Amish read local small-town newspapers. But most everyone also follows the doings of other Amish nationwide through The Budget *(above)*, based in Sugarcreek, Ohio, and sold in Amish communities around the country. Amish people read English and German bibles *(opposite)*; those used in services are written in High German.

Amish cemeteries (opposite and above) are found in fields away from any church. Headstones are relatively uniform in design as it is considered sinful to set oneself apart from another, even in death. Many headstones attest to the long lives of many hard-working Amish people. Life in rural Amish country (overleaf) is picture-postcard neat, efficiently organized, and serenely peaceful. The toil is hard but satisfying, and support is everywhere.

Index

Englishers *can be Amish briefly for a gag photograph, but con-verting to the Amish way of life is difficult and rarely accom-plished. Those who have tried and failed say they missed, more than anything, their automobiles and the freedom of movement.*

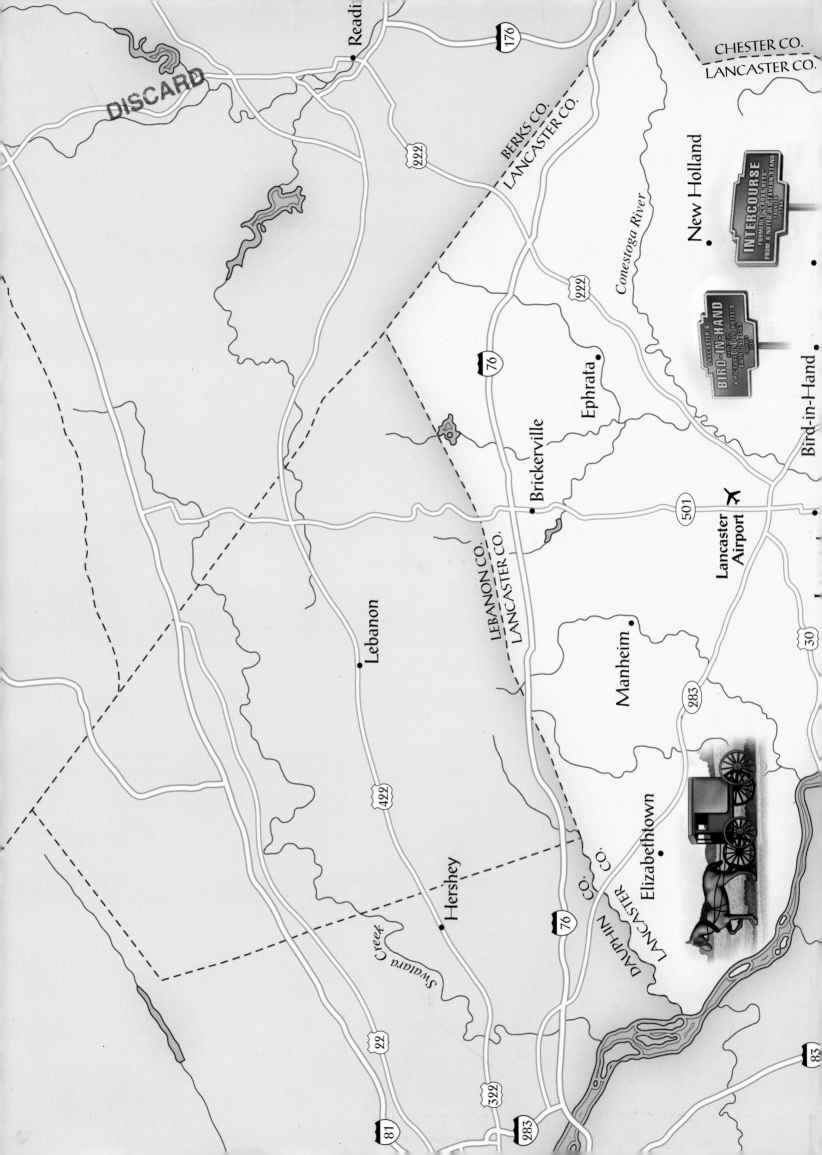